Made in the USA
Coppell, TX
10 February 2022

73264058R00057